The Hidden Valley Walk

A Valley Walk Through Pendle Country

A 22-mile circular walk from Whalley to Blacko and return

David Phipps

Palatine Books, 1994

For Sandra, Heath and Leona

NB. Whilst every care is taken in the preparation of this book to ensure accuracy, walkers are advised to make use of the appropriate Ordnance Survey maps to locate precise routes. Please keep to the authorised footpaths described in the text and respect the privacy of the residents whose properties you pass on your way.

For the benefit of future walkers please notify any footpath obstructions to the County Surveyor and Bridgemaster, County Hall, Preston.

The Hidden Valley Walk
David Phipps

Published by Palatine Books, an imprint of Carnegie Publishing Ltd.,
18 Maynard St, Preston

Typeset in Monotype Ehrhardt by Carnegie Publishing
Printed in the UK by T. Snape & Co. Ltd, Preston

ISBN 1-874181-06-3

Contents

	Foreword	*vii*
Section One	Whalley To Spring Wood Picnic Site (1 mile)	1
Section Two	Spring Wood to Nick of Pendle (2¼ miles)	4
Section Three	Nick of Pendle to Sabden Fold (2¼ miles)	7
Section Four	Sabden Fold to Bull Hole Lane (½ mile)	9
Section Five	Bull Hole Lane to Newchurch (½ mile)	11
Section Six	Newchurch to Whitehough (1¼ miles)	12
Section Seven	Whitehough to Stang Top Road (¾ mile)	15
Section Eight	Stang Top Road to Blacko (2 miles)	16
Section Nine	From Blacko to Blacko Tower (2 miles return)	20
Section Ten	Blacko to Sabden (6 miles)	21
Section Eleven	Sabden to Spring Wood Picnic Site (2½ miles)	26
Section Twelve	Spring Wood Picnic Site to Whalley (1 mile)	30

One of the gatehouses at Whalley Abbey

Foreword

I HAVE LIVED in the Burnley area for some twenty-nine years and, more latterly, in the Pendle area for about fifteen years. I have always enjoyed walking but only began 'serious' walking about ten years ago. By 'serious' I mean that it became my main hobby and enjoyment, probably prompted by living so close to the beauties of the Pendleside area.

Many 'walk books' concentrate on the Lake District and Yorkshire Dales which are, of course, areas of great natural beauty. However, to me, the delights of the Pendleside area can match them in lots of ways. Imagine the delights that the names of places like Ratten Clough, Bull Hole, Roughlee, Blacko, Noggarth, Stang Top and Nanny Mauds can invoke.

The idea to write my own walk has been brewing in my mind for some time now but only really started to take shape whilst walking the many paths of the Sabden Valley. It was here that I realised there was the potential for a moderate length walk with an interesting goal to aim for.

The whole walk is approximately twenty-two miles long and can, I suppose, be completed in one longish day by the 'head-down-see-nothing' brigade. Alternatively, the walk can easily be shortened to about eighteen miles by starting at Spring Wood picnic site and missing out the visit to Blacko Tower. Nowhere along its route are there any steep hills or climbs worth mentioning.

Ideally, the aim of the book is to entice walkers to the area for a two-day walk with an overnight stay at Blacko (or, just down the road, Barrowford and Nelson) so that the walk can be completed at a more leisurely pace and enable the walker to enjoy this beautiful corner of Lancashire.

If, on planning the walk, difficulties are experienced in gaining overnight accommodation at the Blacko end of the walk, an alternative would be to commence at Blacko and stay overnight at Whalley or Clitheroe, where accommodation is more plentiful. Parking in Blacko is somewhat limited, but the friendly host of The Rising Sun Inn will usually allow his car park to be utilised by those who seek permission.

In the text of the book I have included six 'escape routes' which would enable the walker to cut the walk short should he or she find that they were running out of time, or the weather turned bad. Additionally, they can be used to complete the whole of the walk in six short 'rambles'.

Accommodation

Accommodation is somewhat limited at Blacko and at the time of writing there are only two places that provide bed and breakfast in Blacko itself. Barrowford (about 1½ miles) is also somewhat limited, but Nelson (about 3 miles) has more to offer. Both towns are on a main bus route. Accommodation lists can be obtained from the Tourist Information Centres at 20 Scotland Road, Nelson (tel. 0282 692890) and 12/14 Market Place, Clitheroe (tel. 0200-25566), or by consulting the Yellow Pages.

Transport

Bus Passenger Enquiries: Burnley and Pendle Transport, tel. 0282–425244. Train Passenger Enquiries: British Rail, Burnley, tel. 0282–425421.

Walkers are advised to telephone Clitheroe Police Station (tel. 0200–23818) if they intend to leave their car overnight at Whalley. Please do not leave any valuables in the car.

Maps

The sketch map in this book is intended only for general guidance. Please make use of Ordnance Survey Pathfinder Maps, SD 63/73, SD 83/93 and SD 84/94, or Landranger Sheet 103.

Section One

Whalley To Spring Wood Picnic Site

WHALLEY, apart from its famous church and abbey, is well worth exploring before setting off on the walk. There are several quiet backwaters that contain both Tudor and Georgian houses, and tea shops and other facilities abound.

The parish church is full of interesting items, including stained glass windows bearing the heraldic shields of the important families of the area: Townley, Parker, Assheton, Nowell, Starkie and others. In the churchyard is a gravestone dated 1856 and inscribed:

> Spectators all, as ye pass by,
> As you are now, so once was I,
> As I am now, so you will be,
> Prepare for death and follow me.

Not a very cheering thought before setting off on a lovely walk, but very true nonetheless!

Whalley Abbey, with its two very imposing gateways, is of the Cistercian order. It was originally founded in Stanlaw, Cheshire, in 1178 but

Whalley Old Grammar School

moved to Whalley in 1296 after first flood and then fire had all but destroyed the original abbey. I wonder if the monks thought a divine message was being sent to them?

From the car park in Whalley centre walk along the main street towards Clitheroe. Turn right on to Brookes Lane (opposite the road to Mitton, Hodder Bridge and Whitewell).

This is one of the many lovely quiet backwaters of Whalley with some fine houses, both old and new. At the top on the left, next door to the seventeenth-century manor house, is the farm Lawsonsteads. The walls of the barn clearly display stonework from Whalley Abbey. At the rear of the farm is a collection of old farm machinery purchased over the years at various farm sales and now painted and looked after by the farmer's wife as a hobby.

Bear to the right through the little wooden gate near a small stone bridge. Follow the track by the brook up to a stile (ignoring a set of two gates half-way along the track). Over the stile, and, almost immediately, a second one, emerging on to open grassland. Walk on with the brook now on your left and follow the left-hand fence and woods to find, at the top of the field, a stile that takes you out on to the Whalley by-pass (A671). Cross the by-pass to Spring Wood picnic site.

Before crossing the by-pass, look back for views of Kemple End (also known as Birdy Brow), and Stoneyhurst College to its left. Enter the picnic site, an ideal spot to examine the tourist information boards.

Spring Wood to Nick of Pendle

FROM SPRING WOOD picnic site, Whalley (where there are toilets, tourist information map and a refreshment bar at weekends/public holidays), turn left towards Burnley/Accrington/Great Harwood. About forty yards on the left is a gap in a stone wall marked by a public footpath signpost. Walk up the left-hand side of the golf course, with the trees and picnic site on your left. Look for a green and white 'footpath' sign on your left, where the golf course widens a little, and follow this sign over a stone slab footbridge and over a wooden stile into a field. From the stile, head off at an angle of about 'ten past the hour' towards the third oak tree from the left, joining the fence coming from the left. Continue to climb steadily up this field, keeping close to the left-hand fence and gradually leaving behind the golf course and club house to your right. (Looking back, there is a superb view of Whalley Nab.) Almost at the top of this field is a stile over the left-hand fence and after crossing this follow the short section of dry stone wall on your right to another wooden stile which you also cross. Immediately on the right is another wooden stile, and you cross this also.

Immediately in front of you is a derelict barn, which is a good view point from which to look back down the Ribble Valley with the tower blocks of Preston in the far distance.

After crossing this last stile, follow the wall to your right.

This is the wall of the Georgian mansion house, Clerk Hill, which was built by the Whalley family between 1715 and 1772. An earlier house on this site was the home of John Hammond, who tortured the Catholic priest Edmund Campion.

This will bring you to a gate with a gap-stile to its left. Through this, and turn left on to the tarmaced lane which serves the rear of the house.

By the side of this gate is a rather nice outbuilding with an initialled datestone, 'J. W. 1772'.

Follow this lane to join another quiet tarmaced lane, where you turn left.

Directly in front of you at this point are views of Hambledon Hill with its many TV and communication masts. Also in view, at the time of writing, is the developing multi-million-pound tourist complex at Huncoat Power Station.

Continue up this lane passing the entrances to Lower Clerk Hill and Hollins Farm (your return route) on the right. As you walk along this lane you will see Fence TV mast, far away on your upper right, which you will walk past on the return route. Carry on walking along this lane, passing Wiswell Moor Farm on the right. The tarmac ceases here, but continue to follow the lane, passing Wiswell Moor House and another two farms on your left. After the second farm, a stile to the right of a five-barred gate across the track gives access to Wiswell Moor itself.

At this point 'The Witches' Way', a thirty-mile walk from Rawtenstall to Slaidburn, joins you from the right and continues with you to the Nick of Pendle. The track now becomes rutted but is easily followed, in the same direction as before, heading now towards the dark, looming features of Pendle Hill (1,831 ft/560m).

In 1652 George Fox, the founder of the Quaker movement, climbed Pendle on his way to visit his future wife, Margaret Fell, who lived at Swarthmoor Hall, near Ulverston, Cumbria.

A walk of twenty to thirty minutes along this track, passing through several gates and passing Wilkins Hey Farm and Parsley Barn, will eventually bring you out just below the Nick of Pendle on the Sabden/Clitheroe road.

To your left at the top of the Nick of Pendle, ice cream, drinks and burgers are sold from motor caravans at weekends and holidays. To the right, downhill, is the pretty village of Sabden with shops, pubs, toilets etc. It is only about five or ten minutes' walk there, but double the time returning as the road is very steep.

'Escape Route' One or Circular Walk One

On reaching the main Sabden/Clitheroe road just below the Nick of Pendle, turn right and walk downhill into Sabden village itself (¾mile). Pass Whalley Road on the right and then the White Hart Inn on the left. After crossing Sabden Bridge turn immediately right, and follow on from page 26.

Nick of Pendle to Sabden Fold

TURN RIGHT downhill towards Sabden, but only as far as the first cattle grid. Just before it, on the left, is a track which you follow to a gate with a kissing gate to its right.

Ahead of you is Churn Clough Reservoir with its Waterman's Cottage, around the back of which you will shortly walk.

Pass through the kissing gate and here the main track swings away to the left alongside a wall. Ignore this, and head up the path to the upper right on a faint path that passes a lone hawthorn tree. Continue over a rise with a ditch and then a wall on your left. As you breast the rise, Churn Clough Reservoir looms into view immediately in front of you down below. A wall and a gate are in front of you, with a wall stile to the right of the gate. Cross this and head straight ahead downhill to join the track around the reservoir. Follow this track (with the reservoir to your right) around the reservoir to Waterman's Cottage. Parked here is a caravan, 'The Fisherman's Cabin' which, apart from selling fishing tackle, also sells drinks, snacks, etc. Just before the cottage, and at the end of the wood on your left, a metal gate on the left gives access to open moorland. Go through this gate, but keep to the path close to the side of a grey-painted iron fence to pass the back of the cottage.

At the back of the cottage is a gate with a small wooden kissing gate to its left. Go through this and then go straight ahead across a very narrow field to the wall directly in front of you. (Sabden is directly ahead.) At the wall, turn left and follow it down the field with the wall and then a fence on your right-hand side. Pass through a gate and continue down to the tarmaced farm road in front of you.

This is Ratten Clough Lane, which used to be a main highway between Sabden and Sabden Fold/Newchurch many years ago.

Here turn left and walk up to and straight through the farmyard of Ratten Clough Farm, with its rather nice kitchen garden and greenhouse on the left. At the end of the farmyard go through a metal gate and continue to follow the stony track (still in a north/north-easterly direction). Soon another gate across the track is met, but a stile in the wall to its right saves opening the gate. Continue along the track with the beauties of the Sabden valley opening up to the right.

The ridge to your right is your return route later in the day (or the next day, for walkers who make this a two-day walk).

Pass the ruins of a barn on your right and down below in the valley bottom is Dean Farm (more of this later).

Along the right-hand side of the track a curious mixture of vaccary and dry stone wall now appears for a short time.

The track now bends and descends to the ruins of Stainscombe, a beautiful old farmhouse on your left, which is well worth a look at.

It was built in the 1670s and was formerly the home of the Stevenson family. Nicholas Stevenson of Admergill sold it in the early eighteenth century to John Haydock of Heysandforth (which is now an area of Burnley). Local gossip has it that a family of felt hat makers once lived here. The walls of the porch, with its stone seats set in either side, contain many names and addresses written by walkers over the years. This provides shelter for rainy day refreshments.

Continue to follow the track as it bends to the right downhill. At the bottom of the hill, through a metal gate (ignore the gate on the right), the track fords Woodhouse Brook and passes another abandoned farmhouse, now used as a store. Continue to follow the track, the next section of which can be muddy after rain. Pass through several gates, passing Lower Lane Farm and then the entrance to Old House Farm on the right. The track now becomes a tarmaced road and bends left and passes Sabden Fold Farm (which used to be the Penmor Arabian Stud Farm) and then Ashendean and Green Top Cottage and Farm, into the hamlet of Sabden Fold.

Sabden Great Hall, which is a mixture of sixteenth- and seventeenth-century building, is just to the right. Inside the porch is a datestone, '1577/1877'.

Escape Route Two or Circular Walk Two

On reaching the hamlet of Sabden Fold, turn right and walk downhill past the front of Sabden Great Hall. Continue along this quiet, narrow country lane until reaching Higher Town Farm on the left (½ mile), then follow on from page 24.

Sabden Fold to Bull Hole Lane

AT THE T-JUNCTION turn left (signposted to Newchurch, 1 mile). After about forty to fifty yards a wall stile reached by overgrown steps with a footpath sign is seen on the right. IGNORE this, and take the next wall gap-stile on the right just before the entrance to Sabden Hall Farm and Cappers Farm. Walk straight across this field in front of Sabden Hall Farm (a stone above the front door tells us that it was built in 1898) to the gap-stile in the wall ahead. Go through this and head straight across the field towards Cappers Farm, closing in on the farm track fence on your left. At the end of this fence is a gate with a stile on its left. Go over this, and head straight ahead on the stony track that passes the rear of the farm, between the barn and the farmhouse. IGNORE the tarmaced drive that goes to the right to the front of the farm. Pass the rear of the farm (on your right), with its beautifully restored leaded lights. There is a gate at the rear of the farm with a stile. Over this, and on passing the last building on the right (indoor swimming pool!) another stile will be seen leading into a field. Take this and follow the left-hand hedge and wall, heading towards the next farm and gate. Go through this gate and keep

Pendle Hill from above Newchurch

following the left-hand wall to the next farm (Meadow Top Farm Kennels, with a datestone above the front door, 'I. M. R. 1734).

Another gate leads you into a small enclosure containing a rather fine sycamore tree. Immediately behind this tree is a wooden fence which you should follow round in front of the farmhouse and a gap-stile appears in a small wall ahead of you. Go through this and then follow the left-hand fence across an open field. (The hamlet of Spen Brook, with its mill chimney, appears on your upper right.) Towards the end of the fence, near the corner of the field and by some hawthorn trees, is a small gap-stile (TAKE CARE—EASILY MISSED). Go through this, and now head up a little gulley on the fairly well-trodden path towards the lone white cottage in the middle of the next field (Lower Well Head Cottage). A stile in a fence ahead of you will be found at the far end of a short section of wall. Now head straight across the front of Lower Well Head Cottage, and a stile will be seen at the far end of the garden. Cross this and walk along the gravel drive, but only until it bends away to the left. Straight ahead another stile is taken, and this leads on to the track that comes up from Bull Hole Cottage down below in the valley bottom.

Escape Route Three or Circular Walk Three

After passing the front of Lower Well Head Cottage and emerging on to the track leading to Bull Hole, turn right on to the track itself and follow it past Bull Hole Cottage to Tinedale Farm, where you turn right, and then follow on from page 23 (½ mile).

On the left as you approach Tinedale farm and cottage are the remains of what is strongly thought to be an eighteenth-century factory that was used in the washing and dyeing of wool. Further evidence, in the form of a large stone trough, can be found in the front yard of the farm.

Sabden Great Hall

Faughs Farm and Quarry, near Newchurch

Section Five

Bull Hole Lane to Newchurch

FOLLOW this track up on to the main Sabden Fold/Newchurch road where you turn right and walk the short distance into Newchurch (where there are toilets, pub with accommodation, shop, telephone and tea room).

On the way, Faughs Quarry is passed on the left, opposite Faughs Farm. The quarry contains the effigy of a man who was killed there about the turn of the century; his workmates carved his face into the rock. Enter the quarry and stand right in the centre so that you have rock face on three sides. Using a compass, turn on this spot until facing a magnetic bearing of 140 degrees. The face is at head height from the floor. At Newchurch in Pendle (once called Goldshaw Booth, and known to locals as Kirk, meaning 'church') it would appear that someone, possibly a local witch, has stretched the road: here, a signpost shows Sabden Fold 1¼ miles, while in Sabden Fold the signpost points to Newchurch 1 mile!

Escape Route Four or Circular Walk Four

On reaching Newchurch, turn right on to Spenbrook Road (signposted to Burnley 5¼ miles) and follow it through the hamlet of Spen Brook, past the mill (carpet manufacturers). Continue to follow the road up the hill and around the bend until an opening and cattle grid on the right are reached (signposted Rigg of England Farm and Tinedale Cottage). Then follow on from page 29, ¾ mile.

Newchurch to Whitehough

AT THE JUNCTION turn left and walk past St. Mary's church and graveyard (well worth a look at, even if only for its 'Eye of God' carved into the church tower). Continue past the Old Friendly Inn, dated 1775, now called 'Granny Janny's', which for many years has been a tea room. Newchurch is a very pretty village and won the Best Kept Village Award in 1965, '66, '67, '68 and '79.

At the Y-junction in the centre of the village by the Lamb Inn, take the road, Jinny Lane, to the right signposted to Roughlee 1 mile but, just after the three-storeyed cottages on the left, take the stile on the left into a field and follow the well-worn path towards and into the wood. Follow the higher path through the wood, crossing a broken-down wall half-way through. On emerging from the wood over a stile, head off in an upper half-left direction to join the left-hand wall which you follow to a stile. Straight ahead is your destination of Blacko, with Stansfield Tower on the skyline behind it.

Down in the valley on your right are the Clarion Tea Rooms, well known to local Sunday walkers as a place to eat your own food, purchase a hot drink and warm yourself by a roaring open fire. Seen over Noggarth Ridge on your right are the built-up areas of Colne, Nelson, Brierfield and Burnley. Over the wall on your left, overshadowed by the Big End of Pendle, is the lovely village of Barley and Lower Ogden Reservoir.

Cross the stile and continue to follow the left-hand wall to another stile which is, in fact, a double stile that enables you to cross the wall on your left. After negotiating this double stile, turn right and continue to follow the wall now on your right.

As you walk along this stretch, directly ahead of you on the other hillside, set in the trees, you will see the wooden buildings of Whitehough Camp School, which is an outdoor education centre run by Lancashire County Council, and which is your next destination.

At the end of the wall is a stile through which you emerge on to Heys Lane, an old main route between Barley and Roughlee many years ago. Cross this lane to the gate opposite and another stile to its right gives access to a field. Down below, and directly in front of you at the other end of the field, can be seen a gate giving access to the Barley/Roughlee road. Head straight for this, and a stile on its right takes you on to the road.

The Hidden Valley Walk—General Route Map

to Clitheroe

------ Route of W

Pendleton Village

Nick of Pendle

Church Clough Reservoir

Ratt Clou

A59

Wiswell Moor Houses

Parsley Barn

Escape Route

Waterman's Cottage

Wiswell radio mast

Wilkins Hey

Whalley Road

Sabden

A671

Clerk Hill

Wiswell Moor Farm

Lower Clerk Hill

Hollins Farm

Whittaker's barn

B6246

Whalley

golf course

Read Wood Stables

Roman road

Hoggarth

to Accrington

to Padiham

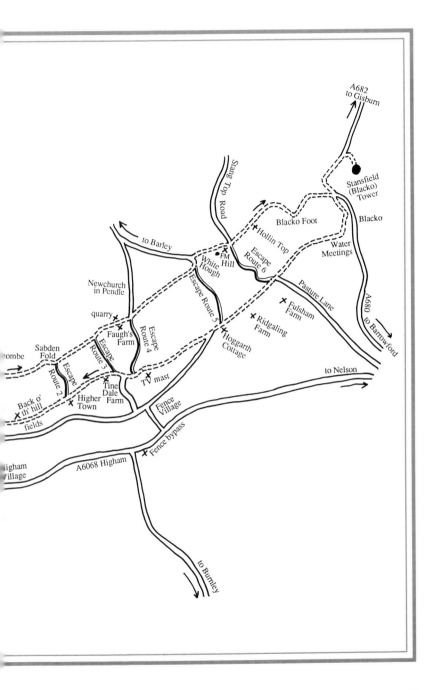

Escape Route Five or Circular Walk Five

On reaching the road at Whitehough, turn right and walk past the rather fine three-storeyed building of Thorneyholme Hall. At the crossroads go straight across, up the hill of Ridge Lane to Noggarth End Road Shop. Now follow on from page 22/23, ¾ mile.

Stansfield (Blacko) Tower and part of Blacko village

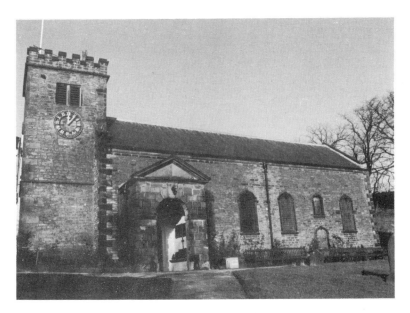

The church at Newchurch

Newchurch village

Whitehough to Stang Top Road

CROSS STRAIGHT OVER and down the cobbled access road to the hamlet of Whitehough. Cross Pendle Water via the bridge and then follow the track to the left, passing the entrance to the fine house, Whitehough Grange, on the right. The track soon splits and you follow the right-hand fork (Yellow Witch Pendle Way sign) between the farm buildings and cottages of Whitehough. Continue to follow this track towards Whitehough Camp School until a small brick building is reached on the right. Here, cross the stile on the right (Pendle Way sign again) and follow the well-worn path through the wood, crossing a small stream by a log bridge. Emerging from the wood, cross the stile in the fence ahead and head directly for the house, Offa Hill, across the field directly ahead, following the left-hand hedge and fence. IGNORE a stile in this fence, but cross a stile (Pendle Way sign) by the side of two gates and head straight for the house, just before which you will find another stile (Pendle Way sign) on your left. Follow the path uphill with a fence on your right to another stile (Pendle Way sign) on the right. Cross this, then follow the fence with concrete posts on your right. At its end, another Pendle Way sign stile takes you down to the right and out on to the farm road leading back to Offa Hill. Turn left and walk to the tarmaced lane, Stang Top Road.

Escape Route Six or Circular Walk Six

After circumnavigating the path around Offa Hill house and walking down the farm track to the tarmaced Stang Top Road, turn right and walk downhill past the caravan site on your right, into Roughlee village. At the T–junction turn right, pass the Bay Horse Inn and turn left over the bridge over Pendle Water, on to Pasture Lane (signposted to Barrowford 1¼ miles). Climb up Pasture Lane, passing Roughlee Fishing Lodge (trout fishing) and then Pendle Valley caravan park on your right. Continue to climb up Pasture Lane towards Barrowford until, at the top of the hill, a tarmaced lane goes off to the right (signposted Fulshaw Farm Dairies and Ridgling Farm). Here turn right and then follow on from page 22.

Section Eight

Stang Top Road to Blacko

TURN left on to this very narrow, quiet country lane and walk uphill a short distance to the track on the right leading to Hollin Top Farm (Pendle Way sign). Walk towards the farm, taking the lower right-hand track when it divides. Soon another Pendle Way sign is seen on the right, but IGNORE this and keep to the farm track.

Down below in the valley can be seen the rear of Roughlee Hall, once the home of Alice Nutter, one of the Pendle witches executed at Lancaster Castle in the seventeenth century.

On reaching the farm a gate will be seen to the left; there is a stile in a short section of wall to its left. Over this, and on to a track that takes you past the rear of the farm. A path now descends to a stile in another wall across the path IGNORE gate to the left into a field and head for the barn in front of you, following the left-hand wall. A stile in the wall to the right of a gate will be found. Over this, and cross into the barn enclosure. (Stansfield Tower lies directly ahead now.) Pass in front of the barn, and three gateways will be seen in front of you. Take the middle one and follow the

Roughlee Hall, Roughlee

right-hand wall, still heading for the tower. A paving of old stones sets you off initially, and then peters out. Keep heading for the tower, and an old iron gate appears in a wall ahead. Go through the gap–stile at this gate, descend the hill following the line of overhead cables. (Bankend House on right, complete with peacocks and other birds.) A small, narrow stile will be found in the wall ahead. Through this, and head straight across the lawned area to cross the driveway to a stile in a small wooden fence just to the left of an old stone gatepost. Still going downhill, cross the field to the bottom left-hand corner, where an old wooden stile takes you out on to the driveway of the house near to a cattle grid. Walk down the driveway to the road (Roughlee to Blacko road) where Blacko Foot Farm is situated. Here turn left and walk along this quiet country lane.

After about ¼ mile a farm track on the right with a cattle grid and public footpath sign is found. Follow this track straight through the farmyard (two gates), pass the farm on the right, cottages on the left and the manor house on the right. Where the track bends to the left, look for a small gate on the right, with a stile (marked 'Dogs must be kept on a lead') and follow the small left-hand wall and hedge past the back of the mill and pond to a wooden stile in a fence at the far end of the mill. Cross the lane to a gap–stile in the wall. Head directly across the next field towards a farm, following a sunken way, to find a stile almost hidden in the hedge ahead. Cross the farm track and go to the left of the barn (black and white footpath sign fixed here on side of barn). After passing the back of the barn and then the house, look for a small gap–stile in the little wall ahead of you. (DO NOT GO TO THE LEFT OF THE HEDGE.) Through this gap–stile and follow the hedge, now on your left, to a wooden stile in the fence ahead of you.

Keep following the left-hand hedge and fence to a gate and metal tubular railings, where a stile will be found at the left-hand side of the gate. Continue straight ahead with the hedge/fence now on your right, on a well-trodden path down to a small stone footbridge and stile. Up ahead, across the next field, will be seen the back of a row of cottages. Head for them and on nearing them a gap–stile will be seen in the wall of the third cottage from the right. This gives access to the track at the back of the cottages and you follow this to the right (taking care to avoid the washing usually hung out at the rear of these cottages!), up on to the main road in Blacko village itself, emerging almost opposite the Rising Sun Inn on the main Nelson/Gisburn road. Food, drinks, etc., can be obtained here.

Section Nine

From Blacko to Blacko Tower

ON REACHING the main Nelson/Gisburn road, turn left and walk towards Gisburn up through Blacko village. Follow a sharp right-hand bend in the road and walk on until the gate of Tower Farm is reached on the right. Go through the gate and follow the farm track up to the farm itself. A gate will be seen on the right; go through this and follow the right-hand wall to a stile. Over this, and then head straight up the hill to Blacko Tower.

This tower was built by Jonathan Stansfield (1823–1894) around 1890. It was originally known as Jonathan's Tower, but is now more widely known as Blacko Tower. He was asked why he was building it and replied, 'I've never drunk or smoked in my life, so I'm making this as my hobby,' although some records state that he built it because the Black Hill (which is what 'Blacko' means) was not high enough at 1,018 feet to enable him to see over the surrounding hills into Ribblesdale. However, when the tower was finished it was still too short.

This section of the walk across Tower Farm to Blacko Tower is not a public right of way and permission to include this section in the book has been granted by the farmer. For this right to be continued in the future, walkers are asked to take every care to observe the Country Code and close all gates, leave no litter, etc.

Section Ten

Blacko to Sabden

TURN right, passing a rather futuristic house on the right with its round turret-like tower. Just before the shop/post office, a track signposted to Water Meetings is taken and followed to Pendle Water. (Water Meetings is a joining of Blacko Water and Pendle Water at Watermeetings Farm.) Cross the bridge, ignoring the Pendle Way sign before it. Just before the farm, by the side of a gate on your right is a clearly marked gap-stile. Go through this and follow Pendle Water upstream with the water and fence on your right. When a hedge comes out of the right hand fence and a dip in the ground is met, bear left (take care here) and walk around this dip. The path becomes much more distinct now, and is followed uphill through the trees and through a gap-stile in a fence. (Good view now, to the right, of Blacko and the tower.)

On emerging from the trees, follow the path to a stile in a fence ahead. Follow the well-worn path alongside the right-hand fence/line of trees which, after a short distance, becomes a wall. Over to your right are Bank End House and Blacko Foot Farm, past which you walked earlier.) You are now heading directly back towards Sabden and Whalley, from where you started. At the wall is a gateway and stile which you go over and then continue in the same direction with the wall now on your left, with the top of Fence TV mast directly ahead. Over a stone step-stile next to a gate, continue to follow the left-hand fence and hedge until a gate and stile are met. This gives access to Pasture Lane, the main road between Barrowford and Roughlee. Cross this and take the tarmaced farm road signposted to Fulshaw Farm Dairies and Ridgling Farm. (Along here are grand views of the Sabden valley with the mill chimney of Spen Brook ahead, Newchurch upper right and Roughlee down to the right with Pendle Hill behind.)

Where the track splits, follow the right-hand one signposted to Ridgling Farm, passing a small reservoir on the left. Here the track splits again; take the right-hand fork directly in front of you, continuing to head south/south-west as before, with the towns of Colne, Nelson and Burnley on your left. When two gates are met, take the right-hand one but IGNORE the track heading off to the right and continue dead ahead, following the left-hand wall with Fence TV mast once again appearing before you, to emerge via a stile at Noggarth End Road Shop, which used to be a toll house (usually open at weekends, etc., for ices, drinks and so on). Here, follow the road to the left (straight ahead, really), but only until the first gate and stile on the right are reached. Over the stile and now head diagonally across the field to the wall end ahead (directly towards Newchurch on the hill on the other side of the valley). On reaching the wall corner end, turn left and head past the static caravan on your left with its little fenced-off garden (what a grand view the occupants have), to the double stile on the other side of the field. Over the stiles, cross the track and head off slightly left across the field in front of you to a gate with a small wooden stile to its left. Over this stile follow the right-hand wall (keep heading towards Fence TV mast), crossing several fields and lines of rocks across your path, until eventually a wall is reached with a small step-stile and gate. Over this, follow the right-hand fence across the next field to a wall-stile in the corner near a lone hawthorn bush. In the next field, follow the right-hand fence to a stile in the fence ahead. Now follow the fence on your left past the back of a farm to a small wooden stile in the fence ahead. With the TV mast now almost in touching distance, a wall and farm appear in front of you. Head to the right-hand end and pass between the wall and a fenced-off pond on the right. Here, join a well-worn path parallel with the left-hand wall (passing the TV mast on your left) that leads to a gate with a small gap stile on its right. Over this, and continue on to Top O'Hill Cottages, where a small footpath gate on the left of a metal farm gate gives access to the track between the cottages and their gardens, and out on to Spen Brook Road.

This is the main road between Fence and Newchurch. Many years ago it was known as Nanny Mauds, as an old woman of that name lived at one of the cottages and was reputed to be imbued with witchcraft powers. With her evil eye she would demand food, etc., from passersby, usually very successfully.

Here turn left (straight ahead, really) and walk up the road, but only as far as the first opening and cattle grid on the right, signposted to Rigg of England Farm and Tinedale Cottage. Over the cattle grid and follow the track (ignore track that swings off to the left and keep to track that follows the right-hand fence and wall) past the cottage and farm (now derelict) on your right. (Between the two buildings, another Pendle Way sign will be seen pointing off down Bull Hole Lane.) After the last of the farm buildings, pick up the wall ahead of you and follow on with the wall on your right to a wooden double stile (and another Pendle Way sign).

I was sitting on this stile one day in July 1990, having a coffee, when a fox loped past within five yards of me. Fortunately, my little dog was busy investigating some rabbit smells on the other side of the wall, and never saw the fox.

Over the stile, follow the left-hand fence to another stile to the right of a gate. Over this, follow the right-hand wall, still in the same south/south-westerly direction. (View of Preston ahead far down the valley.) A gate gives access to the walled track leading into Higher Town Farm yard (noisy dogs!) and thence out on to the Sabden Fold Road. Go straight ahead along this road, but only as far as the first farm track on the right (gate and cattle grid and bridlepath sign). Here, just to the left of the cattle grid, is a wooden stile which you should cross and head off across the field diagonally towards wooded Black Hill, and Preston in the far distance. Lowerhouses Farm lies down to your right. Pass between two fenced-off and covered mine shafts. Walk along the lower slopes of the rocky hill on your left until a wall is seen ahead. A wall-stile will be seen part way up the hill; head for this and over it follow the right-hand wall. Just after a gate on the right the path forks, with one swinging away to the left uphill. IGNORE this and continue to follow the rather indistinct rushy path by the wall on your right, heading towards Back O'th'Hill Farm (now called Stone Fold).

An interesting point is that present-day maps show this as Back O'th'Hill Farm, whilst an 1848 map of the area shows it as Back of the

Noggarth End Road shop

Hill, with another farm close by being called Back o' the Hill. No trace of this farm now remains.

Pass through a gate and follow the path, now clearer as it passes to the left of the house (which has fenced-off gardens with lots of birds and ponds). As you pass the ponds, a wooden gate appears in front of you. A stile to its left takes you over this and the path is now enclosed between two wire fences. (IGNORE the tall, narrow wire-fenced gate that leads to the house and gardens.) This fenced-in path leads out on to the driveway to the house where you should turn right and walk past the front of the house. Immediately after the house a step-stile in the wall ahead is crossed and a clear 'green way' path is used to cross the next field (Sabden now coming into view ahead of you), down towards a gate where the overhead telephone lines cross a wall. A stile just to the left above the gate gives access to another field, and here the left-hand wall is followed. Just before a gate a step-stile in the left-hand wall is crossed, then walk around the corner of the wall and pass the gate now on your right. Follow the track down to Dean Farm.

Dean Farm is one of the oldest buildings in the Sabden valley, being built in 1574 by the Moore family. Above the lower windows is inscribed, 'This house was builded by Hugh More son of Chrestover More oldest brother son and Letis Hugh wife in the year of our Lord God 1574'.

On reaching the farm, turn left and follow this track along the valley bottom into Sabden, where there are toilets, shops, telephone, pubs, etc.

Section Eleven

Sabden to Spring Wood Picnic Site

ON REACHING Sabden, walk down St. Nicholas Avenue straight ahead of you on to the main (Padiham/Clitheroe) road, passing Sabden Methodist church. On reaching the main road, turn left and over the bridge of Sabden Brook. Turn right immediately after the bridge on to a rough car track that passes some old garages on the right and Brookside house on the left. Follow this track past some rather splendid new and old houses until it emerges on to a tarmaced road with some terraced houses. Here, turn left, walk between the new houses and straight forward on to a track, with the football field on your left. The track now bends right and you are off again in a south/south-westerly direction, with good views of the wooded Black Hill to your left and Sabden to your right.

The track soon passes close by the Pendle Antique Centre. Continue to follow the track (bench seats on left) as it passes two detached bungalows on your right, and then enters open fields. Soon a gate is reached with a stone slab gap-stile to its left. Through this, and continue to follow the track through another gate, passing Whittaker's Barn on your right. The track continues to another gate with a wooden stile to its right. Over this and follow the right-hand fence, but only until it bends away to the right. Here, follow the track as it heads up towards the wood on your left and then bends right to follow the line of the trees. Go through another gate and the track then passes Whittaker's Farm on your right. Here you join the tarmaced drive of the farm which continues ahead and after a short distance emerges at a cattle grid on to the old Roman road. Here turn right and follow the road for a couple of hundred yards to the end of the wood on your right. Here, go through a gate on your right and follow the wall on your right by the side of the wood. Cross a stone step-stile in the wall ahead and then turn left and follow the wall side. When the wall on your left turns away to the left, Read Wood Stables appear ahead. Head straight for them to a gate in the fence ahead of you. A track now appears, which you follow into the yard of Read Wood Stables.

CARE IS NEEDED HERE. On reaching the tarmaced drive of Read Wood Stables, turn right (horse equipment shop on left, metal barn on right). Walk up to the gate to the left of this barn. Now turn left and follow right-hand fence down to a stile leading on to an old sunken way. Over this stile and follow the left-hand wall down the old sunken way. Cross an old broken down wall, and when the wall on your left turns sharply away to the left, continue on ahead on a path that descends through the wood. It soon forks; take the lower left-hand path that still descends through the wood. When it forks again, take the lower left-hand path once again. A fence is reached where the remains of an old broken stile will be found. Over this, and head down across the field to the footbridge with handrails, clearly seen crossing the stream ahead of you. Cross the footbridge and immediately turn left to follow the stream on your left. Again, almost immediately head away from the stream for a point midway between the stream and a telegraph post on your right, which is directly in line with a farmhouse.

Over a small rise, and hidden by it, an old rusty gate will be found in a gap in a line of trees. Just to the right of this gate an old wooden stile will be found. The stile is actually nailed into the large tree. Here a concrete footpath sign is fastened to the other side of the tree. Cross this stile and then, with your back to it, look directly across the field and a wooden ladder-stile will be seen in the hedge/tree line. Cross this ladder-stile and to your upper right the barn of Whittams Farm will be seen. head to the right-hand side of it, virtually following the line of overhead cables. These will lead you to a gate through which you should then follow the left-hand hedge up on to the Whalley/Sabden road at some stone steps and a stile. Cross the road, over another stile and follow the line of trees/hedge/stream on your left. Cross another stile (concrete footpath sign) and continue in the same direction up to Hollins Farm. Pass the farm and, immediately after, a gate on your left allows you to ford the stream and join a rough track. This leads to a gate through which you go to pass the front of Hollins Farm with its stables. Now walk along the tarmaced farm track to reach the road near to Clerk Hill. At the road, turn left and then right on to the rear service road of Clerk Hill house and retrace your steps across the golf course to Spring Wood picnic site.

Section Twelve

Spring Wood Picnic Site to Whalley

AFTER CROSSING Whalley by-pass (A671) from Spring Wood picnic site, go up the tree-lined path and cross the stile. Head off across the open field on a 'green way' path towards Kemple End and Stonyhurst College. The path skirts a little sunken area and then swings off to the left towards Whalley Nab, with its mast on top. A small stile in a fence will be found which leads on to a small wooden step-stile giving access to the road into Whalley (B6246). Cross this road to a stone stile (almost opposite) with a public footpath sign, and on to a hawthorn-lined path. Follow this path down to the River Calder, where the path bears to the right to follow the river downstream past the weir and back into Whalley via another quiet backwater, Calder Vale. Turn right for the car park.

The Country Code

1. Respect the life and work of the countryside.
2. Protect wildlife, plants and trees.
3. Keep to the public paths across farmland.
4. Safeguard water supplies.
5. Go carefully on country roads.
6. Keep dogs under control.
7. Guard against all risk of fire.
8. Fasten all gates.
9. Leave no litter—take it with you.
10. Make no unnecessary noise.
11. Leave livestock, crops and machinery alone.
12. Use gates and stiles to cross fences, hedges and walls.